If found, please return to

_____

_____

_____

_____

Dates and times of meetings in the body of
the Diary and the opening of facilities such
as libraries, museums, and the University
Centre, depend upon the development of
the COVID-19 infection in the autumn and
beyond. It is likely, for a time at least, that
meetings will need to be held remotely by
Zoom or some such device.

The
Cambridge
Pocket Diary

2020–2021

The
Cambridge
Pocket Diary

2020–2021

CAMBRIDGE
UNIVERSITY PRESS

CAMBRIDGE
UNIVERSITY PRESS

University Printing House, Cambridge CB2 8BS, United Kingdom

Cambridge University Press is part of the University of Cambridge.

It furthers the University's mission by disseminating knowledge in the pursuit of education, learning and research at the highest international levels of excellence.

www.cambridge.org
Information on this title: www.cambridge.org/978-1-108-82483-5

© Cambridge University Press 2020

First published 2020

Printed in the United Kingdom by FLB Group Ltd

ISBN 978-1-108-82483-5

CONTENTS

5

2020	S	M	Tu	W	Th	F	S
Oct.	...	...	[6	...	1	2	3
	4	5	6	7	8	9	10
	11	12	13	14	15	16	17
	18	19	20	21	22	23	24
	25	26	27	28	29	30	31
Nov.	1	2	3	4	5	6	7
	8	9	10	11	12	13	14
	15	16	17	18	19	20	21
	22	23	24	25	26	27	28
	29	30	...	...	...	...	...
Dec.	...	...	1	2	3	4]	5
	6	7	8	9	10	11	12
	13	14	15	16	17	18	19
	20	*21*	*22*	*23*	*24*	*25*	*26*
	27	*28**	*29*	*30*	*31*	...	...
2021							
Jan.	...	...	...	...	...	1*	2
	3	4	5	6	7	8	9
	10	11	12	13	14	15	16
	17	18	[19	20	21	22	23
	24	25	26	27	28	29	30
	31	...	...	...	...	...	...
Feb.	...	1	2	3	4	5	6
	7	8	9	10	11	12	13
	14	15	16	17	18	19	20
	21	22	23	24	25	26	27
	28	...	...	...	...	...	...
Mar.	...	1	2	3	4	5	6
	7	8	9	10	11	12	13
	14	15	16	17	18	19]	20
	21	22	23	24	25	*26*	*27*
	28	*29*	*30*	*31*	...	...	...

Vacations are shown by italic figures. First and period of residence are shown by square brackets.

THE YEAR 2020–21

2021	S	M	Tu	W	Th	F	S
APR.	...	...	...	...	1	2	3
	4	5*	6	7	8	9	10
	11	12	13	14	15	16	**17**
	18	**19**	**20**	**21**	**22**	**23**	**24**
	25	**26**	[**27**	**28**	**29**	**30**	...
MAY	...	...	...	...	...	...	**1**
	2	**3***	**4**	**5**	**6**	**7**	**8**
	9	**10**	**11**	**12**	**13**	**14**	**15**
	16	**17**	**18**	**19**	**20**	**21**	**22**
	23	**24**	**25**	**26**	**27**	**28**	**29**
	30	**31***	...	...	...	...	...
JUNE	...	...	**1**	**2**	**3**	**4**	**5**
	6	**7**	**8**	**9**	**10**	**11**	**12**
	13	**14**	**15**	**16**	**17**	**18**]	**19**
	20	**21**	**22**	**23**	**24**	**25**	26
	27	28	29	30	...	...	...
JULY	...	...	...	...	1	2	3
	4	5	6	7	8	9	10
	11	[12	13	14	15	16	17
	18	19	20	21	22	23	24
	25	26	27	28	29	30	31
AUG.	1	2	3	4	5	6	7
	8	9	10	11	12	13	14]
	15	16	17	18	19	20	21
	22	23	24	25	26	27	28
	29	30*	31	...	...	...	...
SEP.	...	...	...	1	2	3	4
	5	6	7	8	9	10	11
	12	13	14	15	16	17	18
	19	20	21	22	23	24	25
	26	27	28	29	30	...	...

last days of Full Term and of the Long Vacation
An asterisk denotes a Bank Holiday.

MICHAELMAS TERM LECTURE-LIST

	Monday	Tuesday	Wednesday	Thursday	Friday	Saturday
9.0–10.0						
10.0–11.0						
11.0–12.0						
12.0–1.0						
1.0–2.0						

2.0–3.0	3.0–4.0	4.0–5.0	5.0–6.0	6.0–7.0

LENT TERM LECTURE-LIST

	Monday	Tuesday	Wednesday	Thursday	Friday	Saturday
9.0–10.0						
10.0–11.0						
11.0–12.0						
12.0–1.0						
1.0–2.0						

2.0–3.0					
3.0–4.0					
4.0–5.0					
5.0–6.0					
6.0–7.0					

EASTER TERM LECTURE-LIST

	Monday	Tuesday	Wednesday	Thursday	Friday	Saturday
9.0–10.0						
10.0–11.0						
11.0–12.0						
12.0–1.0						
1.0–2.0						

2.0–3.0				
3.0–4.0				
4.0–5.0				
5.0–6.0				
6.0–7.0				

S
30

TWELFTH SUNDAY AFTER TRINITY
Sun rises 6.8, sets 7.51

M
31

Bank Holiday
Library closed

Tu
1

Research Period

W 2

Full Moon, 5.22 a.m.

Th 3

F 4

Press Syndicate (Academic Publishing Committee), 2.15

S 5

Research Period

S
6

THIRTEENTH SUNDAY AFTER TRINITY
Sun rises 6.20, sets 7.35

M
7

Tu
8

Research Period

W
9

Th
10

Moon's Last Quarter, 9.26 a.m.

F
11

S
12

Research Period

SEPTEMBER 2020

S
13

FOURTEENTH SUNDAY AFTER TRINITY
Sun rises 6.31, sets 7.18

M
14

Tu
15

Duke of Sussex born, 1984

Research Period

W 16

Th 17
New Moon, 11.0 a.m.
Press & Assessment Board, 1.0

F 18

S 19
Rosh HaShanah (Jewish) begins

Research Period

S
20

FIFTEENTH SUNDAY AFTER TRINITY
Sun rises 6.43, sets 7.2

M
21

ST MATTHEW
Council, 10.15

Tu
22

Research Period

W 23

Th 24 Moon's First Quarter, 1.55 a.m.

F 25 Press Syndicate (Academic Publishing Committee), 2.15
Alumni Festival begins, its programme being online.

S 26

Research Period

**S
27**

SIXTEENTH SUNDAY AFTER TRINITY
Sun rises 6.54, sets 6.45
Alumni Festival ends

**M
28**

Yom Kippur (Jewish)

**Tu
29**

ST MICHAEL AND ALL ANGELS

Research Period

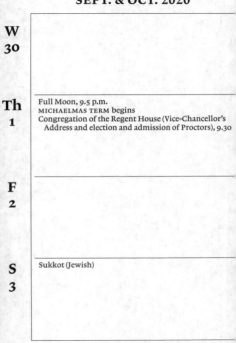

W 30

Th 1
Full Moon, 9.5 p.m.
MICHAELMAS TERM begins
Congregation of the Regent House (Vice-Chancellor's Address and election and admission of Proctors), 9.30

F 2

S 3
Sukkot (Jewish)

Michaelmas Term

S
4

SEVENTEENTH SUNDAY AFTER TRINITY
Sun rises 7.6, sets 6.29

M
5

Board of Engineering, 2.15
Antiquarian Society, 6.0

Tu
6

FULL TERM begins
Board of Business & Management, 2.15
Council of School of Clinical Medicine, 10.30

Michaelmas Term

W **7**	Finance Committee of the Council, 10.15 General Board, 2.0
Th **8**	Audit Committee, 10.15 Board of Education, 3.30 Board of Land Economy, 2.0 Board of Law, 2.30
F **9**	*St Denys* Press Syndicate (Academic Publishing Committee), 2.15
S **10**	Moon's Last Quarter, 12.40 a.m.

Michaelmas Term

OCTOBER 2020

S
11

EIGHTEENTH SUNDAY AFTER TRINITY
Simchat Torah (Jewish)
Sun rises 7.18, sets 6.13
Oxford Full Term begins

M
12

Board of History & Philosophy of Science, 2.30
Board of Modern & Medieval Languages &
   Linguistics, 1.45
Council of School of Biological Sciences, 2.0

Tu
13

Board of Architecture & History of Art, 1.45
Board of Asian & Middle Eastern Studies, 2.0
Board of Clinical Medicine, 10.0
Board of Computer Science & Technology, 2.15
Board of History, 2.15
Natural Sciences Tripos Committee, 2.15
Library Syndicate, 2.0
Discussion, 2.0

Michaelmas Term

W 14

University & Assistants Joint Board, 2.15

Th 15

Board of Divinity, 2.15
Board of Human, Social, & Political Science, 2.0

F 16

New Moon, 7.31 p.m.

S 17

St Etheldreda
Navaratri (Hindu)

Michaelmas Term

S
18

NINETEENTH SUNDAY AFTER TRINITY
ST LUKE
Sun rises 7.30, sets 5.58
Preacher, A. G. Reddie of Wesley House, Extraordinary
Professor of Theological Ethics at the University of South
Africa & Director of the Oxford Centre for Religion and
Culture, 11.15

M
19

Council, 10.15
Board of Biology , 4.15
Board of Economics, 2.0
Philosophical Society Council (and A.G.M.), 4.45

Tu
20

End of first quarter of Michaelmas Term

Michaelmas Term

W
21

Th
22

Board of Classics, 2.0
Board of Mathematics, 2.15
Bursars' Committee, 2.15
Council of School of Physical Sciences, 10.0

F
23

Moon's First Quarter, 1.23 p.m.
Board of Physics & Chemistry, 2.15
Council of School of Humanities & Social Sciences, 2.0
Council of School of Technology, 2.0
Press Syndicate (Academic Publishing Committee), 2.15

S
24

United Nations Day
Congregation of the Regent House, 11.0

Michaelmas Term

S
25

TWENTIETH SUNDAY AFTER TRINITY
Dussehra (Hindu)
Sun rises 6.43, sets 4.43
Summer Time ends

M
26

Tu
27

Board of Earth Sciences & Geography, 2.15
Council of School of Arts & Humanities, 2.0
Discussion, 2.0

Michaelmas Term

OCTOBER 2020

W 28

ST SIMON AND ST JUDE

Th 29

Chemical Engineering & Biotechnology Syndicate, 2.15

F 30

Senior Tutors' Committee, 2.15

S 31

VIGIL
Full Moon, 2.49 p.m.

Michaelmas Term

S 1

TWENTY-FIRST SUNDAY AFTER TRINITY
ALL SAINTS. Scarlet Day
Sun rises 6.56, sets 4.30
Commemoration of Benefactors. Scarlet Day.
  Preacher, S. L. Teather, of St John's College,
  Director of the Jesuit Refugee Service UK
  (*Lady Margaret's Preacher*), 11.15

M 2

All Souls
Antiquarian Society, 6.0

Tu 3

Michaelmas Term

W 4

General Board, 2.0

Th 5

Board of Divinity, 2.15
Board of Law, 2.15
Press & Assessment Board, 1.0
Smuts Fund Managers, 3.30

F 6

Press Syndicate (Academic Publishing Committee), 2.15
Roll of the Regent House and Lists of Faculties
    promulgated

S 7

Michaelmas Term

S 8

TWENTY-SECOND SUNDAY AFTER TRINITY
Remembrance Sunday
Moon's Last Quarter, 1.46 p.m.
Sun rises 7.8, sets 4.18

M 9

Board of Clinical Medicine, and Annual Meeting of the
    Faculty, 1.0
Michaelmas Term divides

Tu 10

Faculty of Computer Science & Technology, Annual
    Meeting of the Faculty, 2.15
Natural Sciences Tripos Committee, 2.15
Discussion, 2.0

Michaelmas Term

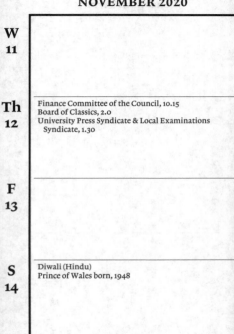

W
11

Th
12

Finance Committee of the Council, 10.15
Board of Classics, 2.0
University Press Syndicate & Local Examinations
 Syndicate, 1.30

F
13

S
14

Diwali (Hindu)
Prince of Wales born, 1948

S
15

TWENTY-THIRD SUNDAY AFTER TRINITY
Nativity Fast (Orthodox) begins
New Moon, 5.7 a.m.
Sun rises 7.21, sets 4.7

M
16

Audit Committee, 10.15
Board of Engineering, 2.15
Board of History & Philosophy of Science, 2.30
Fitzwilliam Museum Syndicate, 2.0
Philosophical Society Council, 4.45

Tu
17

Board of Architecture & History of Art, and Annual
    Meeting of the Faculty, 1.45
Board of Asian & Middle Eastern Studies, and Annual
    Meeting of the Faculty, 2.0
Board of Business & Management, 2.15

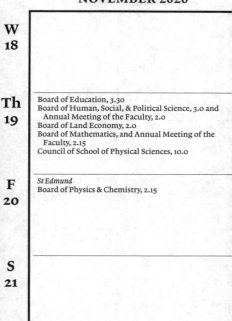

W 18

Th 19

Board of Education, 3.30
Board of Human, Social, & Political Science, 3.0 and
   Annual Meeting of the Faculty, 2.0
Board of Land Economy, 2.0
Board of Mathematics, and Annual Meeting of the
   Faculty, 2.15
Council of School of Physical Sciences, 10.0

F 20

St Edmund
Board of Physics & Chemistry, 2.15

S 21

S
22

TWENTY-FOURTH SUNDAY AFTER TRINITY
St Cecilia
Moon's First Quarter, 4.45 a.m.
Sun rises 7.33, sets 3.58

M
23

Council, 10.15
Board of Economics, 2.0
Council of School of Biological Sciences, 2.0

Tu
24

Meeting of the Faculty, 2.15
Board of Computer Science & Technology, 2.15
Board of Earth Sciences & Geography, and Annual
Meeting of the Faculty, 2.15
Board of History, 2.15
Council of School of Arts & Humanities, 2.0
Council of School of Clinical Medicine, 2.30
Discussion, 2.0

Michaelmas Term

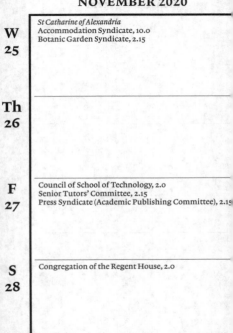

W 25
St Catharine of Alexandria
Accommodation Syndicate, 10.0
Botanic Garden Syndicate, 2.15

Th 26

F 27
Council of School of Technology, 2.0
Senior Tutors' Committee, 2.15
Press Syndicate (Academic Publishing Committee), 2.15

S 28
Congregation of the Regent House, 2.0

Michaelmas Term

S
29

FIRST SUNDAY IN ADVENT
Sun rises 7.44, sets 3.52
End of third quarter of Michaelmas Term

M
30

ST ANDREW
Guru Nanak Birthday (Sikh)
Full Moon, 9.30 a.m.
Board of Modern & Medieval Languages &
  Linguistics, 1.45

Tu
1

St Eligius

Michaelmas Term

DECEMBER 2020

W 2

General Board, 2.0

Th 3

Board of Classics, 2.0
Board of Divinity, 2.15
Board of Law, 2.15

F 4

Council of School of Humanities & Social Sciences, 2.0
FULL TERM ends

S 5

Colleges' Committee, 10.0
Oxford Full Term ends

Michaelmas Term

S 6

SECOND SUNDAY IN ADVENT
Sun rises 7.53, sets 3.48

M 7

Antiquarian Society, 6.0

Tu 8

Moon's Last Quarter, 12.37 a.m.
Discussion, 2.0

Michaelmas Term

W
9

Press & Assessment Board, 2.0

Th
10

F
11

Chanukkah (Jewish)

S
12

Michaelmas Term

DECEMBER 2020

S
13

THIRD SUNDAY IN ADVENT
Sun rises 8.1, sets 3.47

M
14

New Moon, 4.17 p.m.
Council, 10.15

Tu
15

Michaelmas Term

**W
16**

O Sapientia

**Th
17**

**F
18**

**S
19**

MICHAELMAS TERM ends

Michaelmas Term

S
20

FOURTH SUNDAY IN ADVENT
Sun rises 8.6, sets 3.49

M
21

ST THOMAS
Moon's First Quarter, 11.41 p.m.

Tu
22

Christmas Vacation

W
23

Th
24

VIGIL
Library closed

F
25

CHRISTMAS DAY. Scarlet Day
Library closed

S
26

ST STEPHEN
Library closed

Christmas Vacation

S
27

SUNDAY AFTER CHRISTMAS
ST JOHN THE EVANGELIST
Sun rises 8.9, sets 3.53

M
28

INNOCENTS' DAY
Bank Holiday
Library closed

Tu
29

Library closed

Christmas Vacation

W 30

Full Moon, 3.28 a.m.
Library closed

Th 31

Library Closed

F 1

CIRCUMCISION
Bank Holiday
Library Closed

S 2

Library Closed

Christmas Vacation

S
3

SECOND SUNDAY AFTER CHRISTMAS
Sun rises 8.8, sets 4.0

M
4

Antiquarian Society, 6.0

Tu
5

LENT TERM begins

Lent Term

W 6

EPIPHANY
Moon's Last Quarter, 9.37 a.m.

Th 7

F 8

Press Syndicate (Academic Publishing Committee), 2.15

S 9

Duchess of Cambridge born, 1982

Lent Term

S
10

FIRST SUNDAY AFTER EPIPHANY
Sun rises 8.5, sets 4.9

M
11

Tu
12

Lent Term

W
13

New Moon, 5.0 a.m.

Th
14

Makar Sandranti (Hindu)

F
15

S
16

Lent Term

S 17

SECOND SUNDAY AFTER EPIPHANY
Sun rises 7.59, sets 4.20
Oxford Full Term begins

M 18

Council of School of Biological Sciences, 2.0

Tu 19

FULL TERM begins
Board of Business & Management, 2.15
Board of Computer Science & Technology, 2.15
Board of Earth Sciences & Geography, 2.15
Council of School of Clinical Medicine, 10.30

Lent Term

W
20

Moon's First Quarter, 9.2 p.m.
General Board, 2.0

Th
21

Board of Education, 3.30
Board of Law, 3.0

F
22

Board of Physics & Chemistry, 2.15
Press Syndicate (Academic Publishing Committee), 2.15

S
23

S
24

THIRD SUNDAY AFTER EPIPHANY
Sun rises 7.51, sets 4.32
End of first quarter of Lent Term

M
25

CONVERSION OF ST PAUL
Council, 10.15
Board of Economics, 2.0
Board of Engineering, 2.15
Board of History & Philosophy of Science, 2.30
Philosophical Society Council, 4.45

Tu
26

Board of Architecture & History of Art, 1.45
Board of Clinical Medicine, 10.0
Board of History, 2.15
Natural Sciences Tripos Committee, 2.15
Council of School of Arts & Humanities, 2.0
Discussion, 2.0

Lent Term

JANUARY 2021

W 27

Finance Committee of the Council, 10.15

Th 28

Full Moon, 7.16 p.m.
Audit Committee, 10.15
Board of Divinity, 2.15
Board of Human, Social, & Political Science, 2.0
Board of Land Economy, 2.0
Board of Mathematics, 2.15

F 29

S 30

Congregation of the Regent House, 2.0

Lent Term

S
31

SEPTUAGESIMA SUNDAY
Sun rises 7.41, sets 4.45
Preacher, Rt Rev. G. E. Francis - Dehqani, Suffragan
 Bishop of Loughborough 11.15

M
1

VIGIL
Antiquarian Society, 6.0

Tu
2

PURIFICATION OF THE BLESSED VIRGIN MARY
Candlemas
Board of Asian & Middle Eastern Studies, 2.0
Library Syndicate, 2.0

Lent Term

W 3

Th 4
St Gilbert of Sempringham
Moon's Last Quarter, 5.37 p.m.
Board of Classics, 2.0
Council of School of Physical Sciences, 10.0
Chemical Engineering & Biotechnology Syndicate, 2.15

F 5
Council of School of Humanities & Social Sciences, 2.0
Council of School of Technology, 2.0
Press Syndicate (Academic Publishing Committee), 2.15

S 6
Queen's Accession, 1952

S 7

SEXAGESIMA SUNDAY
Sun rises 7.30, sets 4.58

M 8

Board of Biology, 4.15
Board of Modern and Medieval
  Languages and Linguistics, 1.45
Fitzwilliam Museum Syndicate, 2.0

Tu 9

Press & Assessment Board, 1.0
Discussion, 2.0

Lent Term

FEBRUARY 2021

W 10

St Scholastica
Botanic Garden Syndicate, 2.15

Th 11

St Radegund
New Moon, 7.6 p.m.
University & Assistants Joint Board, 2.15
Smuts Fund Managers, 3.30

F 12

Senior Tutors' Committee, 2.15

S 13

Lent Term divides

Lent Term

S
14

QUINQUAGESIMA SUNDAY
St Valentine
Sun rises 7.17, sets 5.11

M
15

Tu
16

Shrove Tuesday
Board of Earth Sciences & Geography, 2.15

Lent Term

W 17

FIRST DAY OF LENT
Ash Wednesday
General Board, 2.0

Th 18

Board of Divinity, 2.15
Board of Land Economy, 2.0
Board of Law, 2.15
Bursars' Committee, 2.15

F 19

Moon's First Quarter, 6.47 p.m.
Duke of York born, 1960
Board of Physics & Chemistry, 2.15
Press Syndicate (Academic Publishing Committee), 2.15

S 20

Lent Term

S
21

FIRST SUNDAY IN LENT
Sun rises 7.2, sets 5.25

M
22

Council, 10.15
Board of Economics, 2.0

Tu
23

VIGIL
Natural Sciences Tripos Committee, 2.15
Discussion, 2.0

Lent Term

W 24

ST MATTHIAS

Th 25

Board of Mathematics, 2.15

F 26

Purim (Jewish)

S 27

Full Moon, 8.17 a.m.
Congregation of the Regent House, 2.0

Lent Term

S
28

SECOND SUNDAY IN LENT
Sun rises 6.47, sets 5.37
Preacher, K. E. Kilby, Bede Professor of Catholic
Theology in the University of Durham, (*Hulsean
Preacher*), 11.15

M
1

St David
Board of Modern & Medieval Languages &
Linguistics, 1.45
Antiquarian Society, 6.0

Tu
2

Board of Asian & Middle Eastern Studies, 2.0
Board of Computer Science & Technology, 2.15

Lent Term

MARCH 2021

W 3

Finance Committee of the Council, 10.15

Th 4

Audit Committee, 10.15
Board of Classics, 2.0
Board of Human, Social, & Political Science, 2.0
Council of School of Physical Sciences, 10.0
End of third quarter of Lent Term

F 5

Press Syndicate (Academic Publishing Committee), 2.15

S 6

St Tibb
Moon's Last Quarter. 1.30 a.m.

Lent Term

MARCH 2021

S 7

THIRD SUNDAY IN LENT
Sun rises 6.32, sets 5.50

M 8

Commonwealth Day
Board of Engineering, 2.15
Board of History & Philosophy of Science, 2.30
Philosophical Society Council, 4.45

Tu 9

Board of Architecture & History of Art, 1.45
Board of Business & Management, 2.15
Press & Assessment Board, 1.0
Council of School of Arts & Humanities, 2.0
Council of School of Clinical Medicine, 2.30
Discussion, 2.0

Lent Term

W 10

Earl of Wessex born, 1964

Th 11

Maha Shrivrathri (Hindu)
Board of Divinity, 2.15
Board of Education, 3.30

F 12

Senior Tutors' Committee, 2.15
Council of School of Technology, 2.0

S 13

New Moon, 10.21 a.m.
Oxford Full Term ends

Lent Term

S
14

FOURTH SUNDAY IN LENT
Sun rises 6.16, sets 6.2

M
15

Board of Clinical Medicine, 1.0

Tu
16

Board of Earth Sciences & Geography, 2.15
Board of History, 2.15

Lent Term

MARCH 2021

W 17

St Patrick
General Board, 2.0
Accommodation Syndicate, 10.0

Th 18

St Edward, King & Martyr
Board of Classics, 2.0
Board of Law, 2.15

F 19

Board of Physics & Chemistry, 2.15
Council of School of Humanities & Social Sciences, 2.0
Press Syndicate (Academic Publishing Committee), 2.15
FULL TERM ends

S 20

Colleges' Committee, 10.0

S
21

FIFTH SUNDAY IN LENT
Passion Sunday
St Benedict
Moon's First Quarter, 2.40 p.m.
Sun rises 6.0, sets 6.15

M
22

Council, 10.15
Council of School of Biological Sciences, 2.0

Tu
23

Discussion, 2.0

Lent Term

W 24

VIGIL

Th 25

ANNUNCIATION OF THE BLESSED VIRGIN MARY,
   or Lady Day
LENT TERM ends

F 26

S 27

Congregation of the Regent House, 11.0

Lent Term

S 28

SUNDAY BEFORE EASTER
Palm Sunday
Pesach (Jewish) begins
Full Moon, 6.48 p.m.
Sun rises 6.43, sets 7.27
Summer Time begins

M 29

Holi (Hindu)
Hola Mohalla (Sikh)

Tu 30

Easter Vacation

W
31

Th
1

Maundy Thursday

F
2

GOOD FRIDAY
Library closed

S
3

EASTER EVE
VIGIL
Library closed

Easter Vacation

S
4

EASTER SUNDAY. Scarlet Day
Moon's Last Quarter, 10.2 a.m.
Sun rises 6.27, sets 7.39

M
5

MONDAY IN EASTER WEEK
Bank Holiday
Library closed

Tu
6

Easter Vacation

W
7

Th
8

F
9

S
10

Congregation of the Regent House, 11.0

Easter Vacation

S
11

FIRST SUNDAY AFTER EASTER
Sun rises 6.11, sets 7.51

M
12

New Moon, 2.31 a.m.
Antiquarian Society (& A.G.M.), 5.54

Tu
13

Ramadan (Islamic) begins
Vaisakhi (Sikh)

Easter Vacation

W
14

Th
15

F
16

S
17

EASTER TERM begins

APRIL 2021

S 18

SECOND SUNDAY AFTER EASTER
Sun rises 5.56, sets 8.3

M 19

Tu 20

Moon's First Quarter, 6.59 a.m.

Easter Term

W 21

Queen Elizabeth II born, 1926

Th 22

F 23

St George
Prince Louis of Cambridge born, 2018
Press Syndicate (Academic Publishing Committee), 2.15

S 24

Easter Term

S
25

THIRD SUNDAY AFTER EASTER
ST MARK
Sun rises 5.41, sets 8.15
Oxford Full Term begins

M
26

Council, 10.15
Board of Modern & Medieval Languages & Linguistics,
   1.45

Tu
27

Full Moon, 3.32 a.m.
FULL TERM begins
Board of Business & Management, 2.15
Board of Computer Science & Technology, 2.15
Board of Earth Sciences & Geography, 2.15
Press & Assessment Board, 1.0
Council of School of Clinical Medicine, 10.30
Mere's Commemoration. Preacher, to be announced,
   11.45

W
28

Th
29

Board of Law, 3.0

F
30

Lag ba-Omer (Jewish)

S
1

ST PHILIP AND ST JAMES
Congregation of the Regent House, 11.0

S
2

FOURTH SUNDAY AFTER EASTER
Sun rises 5.27, sets 8.27
Princess Charlotte of Cambridge born, 2015

M
3

Moon's Last Quarter, 7.50 p.m.
Bank Holiday

Tu
4

Board of Asian & Middle Eastern Studies, 2.0
Board of Clinical Medicine, 10.0
Board of History, 2.15
Library Syndicate, 2.0
Discussion, 2.0
End of first quarter of Easter Term

W 5

Finance Committee of Council, 10.15
General Board, 2.0

Th 6

St John Evang. ante Portam Latinam
Board of Classics, 2.0
Board of Divinity, 2.15
Board of Education, 3.30
Board of Land Economy, 2.0
Board of Mathematics, 2.15

F 7

Press Syndicate (Academic Publishing Committee), 2.15

S 8

S
9

FIFTH SUNDAY AFTER EASTER
Rogation Sunday
Sun rises 5.14, sets 8.39

M
10

Board of Economics, 2.0
Board of History & Philosophy of Science, 2.30
Fitzwilliam Museum Syndicate, 2.0
Antiquarian Society, 6.0
Philosophical Society Council, 4.45

Tu
11

New Moon, 7.0 p.m.
Natural Sciences Tripos Committee, 2.15
Council of School of Arts & Humanities, 2.0

W 12

University & Assistants Joint Board, 2.15

Th 13

ASCENSION DAY. Scarlet Day
Eid ul-Fitr (Islamic)
Audit Committee, 10.15
Board of Human, Social, & Political Science, 2.0
Council of School of Physical Sciences, 10.0
Chemical Engineering & Biotechnology Syndicate, 2.15
Smuts Fund Managers, 3.30

F 14

Council of School of Humanities & Social Sciences, 2.0
Council of School of Technology, 2.0

S 15

S
16

SUNDAY AFTER ASCENSION DAY
Sun rises 5.3, sets 8.50

M
17

Shavuot (Jewish) begins
Board of Engineering, 2.15

Tu
18

Board of Architecture & History of Art, 1.45
Discussion, 2.0

W 19

Buddha Day
Moon's First Quarter, 7.13 p.m.
Botanic Garden Syndicate, 2.15

Th 20

Board of Law, 2.15

F 21

Board of Physics & Chemistry, 2.15
Senior Tutors' Committee, 2.15
Press Syndicate (Academic Publishing Committee), 2.15
Easter Term divides

S 22

Congregation of the Regent House, 10.0

Easter Term

S
23

WHITSUNDAY. Scarlet Day
Sun rises 4.54, sets 9.0
Preacher to be announced, 11.15 (*Ramsden Preacher*)

M
24

Council, 10.15
Council of School of Biological Sciences, 2.0

Tu
25

Board of Business & Management, 2.15
Board of Earth Sciences & Geography, 2.15
Council of School of Clinical Medicine, 2.30
University Press Syndicate & Local Examinations
  Syndicate, 1.30

W
26

Full Moon, 11.14 a.m.

Th
27

The Venerable Bede
Board of Classics, 2.0
Board of Divinity, 2.15
Board of Mathematics, 2.15
Bursars' Committee, 2.15

F
28

S
29

Easter Term

S
30

TRINITY SUNDAY. Scarlet Day
Sun rises 4.46, sets 9.9

M
31

Bank Holiday

Tu
1

Discussion, 2.0

W 2

Moon's Last Quarter, 7.24 a.m.
CORONATION OF QUEEN ELIZABETH II, 1953

Th 3

Corpus Christi

F 4

Press Syndicate (Academic Publishing Committee), 2.15

S 5

Colleges' Committee, 10.0

S 6

FIRST SUNDAY AFTER TRINITY
Sun rises 4.41, sets 9.16

M 7

Board of Biology, 4.15
Board of Clinical Medicine, 1.0
Board of Economics, 2.0

Tu 8

Board of Asian & Middle Eastern Studies, 2.0
Press & Assessment Board, 1.0
End of third quarter of Easter Term

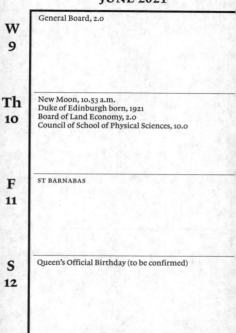

JUNE 2021

W 9
General Board, 2.0

Th 10
New Moon, 10.53 a.m.
Duke of Edinburgh born, 1921
Board of Land Economy, 2.0
Council of School of Physical Sciences, 10.0

F 11
ST BARNABAS

S 12
Queen's Official Birthday (to be confirmed)

S
13

SECOND SUNDAY AFTER TRINITY
Sun rises 4.38, sets 9.21

M
14

Tu
15

Board of Earth Sciences & Geography, 2.15
Council of School of Arts & Humanities, 2.0
Discussion, 2.0

Easter Term

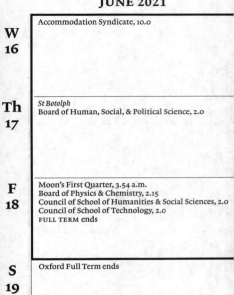

JUNE 2021

W 16

Accommodation Syndicate, 10.0

Th 17

St Botolph
Board of Human, Social, & Political Science, 2.0

F 18

Moon's First Quarter, 3.54 a.m.
Board of Physics & Chemistry, 2.15
Council of School of Humanities & Social Sciences, 2.0
Council of School of Technology, 2.0
FULL TERM ends

S 19

Oxford Full Term ends

JUNE 2021

S
20

THIRD SUNDAY AFTER TRINITY
Sun rises 4.38, sets 9.24

M
21

Duke of Cambridge born, 1982
Council, 10.15
Board of Engineering, 2.15
Board of Modern & Medieval Languages & Linguistics,
1.45

Tu
22

Board of History, 2.15
Discussion, 2.0

Easter Term

JUNE 2021

W
23

VIGIL
Congregation of the Regent House (Honorary
    Degrees), 2.45

Th
24

ST JOHN BAPTIST
Full Moon, 6.40 p.m.
Midsummer
Board of Education, 3.30
Bursars' Committee, 2.15

F
25

EASTER TERM ends

S
26

S
27

FOURTH SUNDAY AFTER TRINITY
Sun rises 4.40, sets 9.25

M
28

VIGIL
Board of History & Philosophy of Science, 2.30

Tu
29

ST PETER
Board of Architecture & History of Art, 1.45
Board of Computer Science & Technology, 2.15
Board of Law, 2.0
Council of School of Clinical Medicine, 10.30

Research Period

JUNE & JULY 2021

W
30

Congregations of the Regent House
  (General Admission)
Scarlet Day

Th
1

Moon's Last Quarter, 9.11 p.m.
Audit Committee, 10.15
Board of Classics, 10.0
Board of Divinity, 2.15
Congregations of the Regent House
  (General Admission)
Scarlet Day

F
2

Press Syndicate (Academic Publishing Committee), 2.15
Congregations of the Regent House
  (General Admission)
Scarlet Day

S
3

Congregations of the Regent House
  (General Admission)
Scarlet Day

Research Period

JULY 2021

S 4

FIFTH SUNDAY AFTER TRINITY
Sun rises 4.45, sets 9.22

M 5

Philosophical Society Council, 4.45

Tu 6

Board of Business & Management, 9.30
Board of Classics, 10.0

Research Period

W
7

Th
8

F
9

S
10

New Moon, 1.17 a.m.
Colleges' Committee, 10.0

Research Period

S
11

SIXTH SUNDAY AFTER TRINITY
Sun rises 4.52, sets 9.18

M
12

Board of Engineering, 2.15
Council of School of Biological Sciences, 2.0
Taught summer courses begin not earlier than this day

Tu
13

Natural Sciences Tripos Committee, 2.15
Discussion, 2.0

Research Period

W 14
Finance Committee of the Council, 10.15
General Board, 2.0
Botanic Garden Syndicate, 2.15

Th 15
St Swithin
Press & Assessment Board, 1.0

F 16
Senior Tutors' Committee, 2.15

S 17
Moon's First Quarter, 10.11 a.m.
Duchess of Cornwall born, 1947

Research Period

S 18

SEVENTH SUNDAY AFTER TRINITY
Sun rises 5.0, sets 9.10

M 19

Council, 10.15

Tu 20

Eid ul-Adha (Islamic)
Board of Clinical Medicine, 10.0

Research Period

W
21

Th
22

St Mary Magdalene
Prince George of Cambridge born, 2013

F
23

Congregation of the Regent House, 10.0

S
24

VIGIL
Full Moon, 2.37 a.m.
Congregation of the Regent House, 10.0

Research Period

S
25

EIGHTH SUNDAY AFTER TRINITY
ST JAMES
Sun rises 5.10, sets 9.1

M
26

Tu
27

Research Period

W
28

Th
29

F
30

Press Syndicate (Academic Publishing Committee), 2.15

S
31

Moon's Last Quarter, 1.16 p.m.

Research Period

S
1

NINTH SUNDAY AFTER TRINITY
Dormition Fast (Orthodox) begins
Sun rises 5.21, sets 8.50

M
2

Tu
3

Research Period

W
4

Th
5

F
6

S
7

Research Period

S
8

TENTH SUNDAY AFTER TRINITY
New Moon, 1.50 p.m.
Sun rises 5.32, sets 8.37

M
9

Tu
10

Al Hijira (Islamic)

Research Period

W
11

Th
12

F
13

S
14

Taught summer courses end not later than this day

Research Period

S
15

ELEVENTH SUNDAY AFTER TRINITY
Dormition (Orthodox)
Moon's First Quarter, 3.20 p.m.
Princess Royal born, 1950
Sun rises 5.43, sets 8.24

M
16

Tu
17

Research Period

W
18

Th
19

F
20

S
21

Research Period

S
22

TWELFTH SUNDAY AFTER TRINITY
Full Moon, 12.2 p.m.
Sun rises 5.55, sets 8.9

M
23

VIGIL

Tu
24

ST BARTHOLOMEW

Research Period

W
25

Th
26

F
27

S
28

St Augustine of Hippo

Research Period

S
29

THIRTEENTH SUNDAY AFTER TRINITY
Sun rises 6.6, sets 7.53

M
30

Moon's Last Quarter, 7.13 a.m.
Bank Holiday
Library closed

Tu
31

Research Period

W
1

Th
2

F
3

Press Syndicate (Academic Publishing Committee), 2.15

S
4

Research Period

S
5

FOURTEENTH SUNDAY AFTER TRINITY
Sun rises 6.18, sets 7.37

M
6

Tu
7

Rosh HaShanah (Jewish) begins
New Moon, 12.52 a.m.

Research Period

W
8

Th
9

F
10

S
11

Research Period

S
12

FIFTEENTH SUNDAY AFTER TRINITY
Sun rises 6.29, sets 7.21

M
13

Moon's First Quarter, 8.39 p.m.

Tu
14

Research Period

W 15

Duke of Sussex born, 1984

Th 16

Yom Kippur (Jewish)

F 17

S 18

Research Period

S 19

SIXTEENTH SUNDAY AFTER TRINITY
Sun rises 6.41, sets 7.5

M 20

VIGIL
Full Moon, 11.55 p.m.
Council, 10.15

Tu 21

ST MATTHEW
Sukkot (Jewish) begins

Research Period

W
22

Th
23

Press & Assessment Board, 1.0

F
24

Press Syndicate (Academic Publishing Committee), 2.15
Alumni Festival begins

S
25

Research Period

S
26

SEVENTEENTH SUNDAY AFTER TRINITY
Sun rises 6.52, sets 6.48
Alumni Festival ends

M
27

Tu
28

Research Period

W
29

ST MICHAEL AND ALL ANGELS
Moon's Last Quarter, 1.57 a.m.

Th
30

F
1

MICHAELMAS TERM begins
Congregation of the Regent House (Vice-Chancellor's
Address and election and admission of Proctors), 9.30

S
2

Michaelmas Term

S 3

EIGHTEENTH SUNDAY AFTER TRINITY
Sun rises 7.4, sets 6.32

M 4

Tu 5

FULL TERM begins

W 6 — New Moon, 11.5 a.m.

Th 7 — Navarathri (Hindu) begins

F 8

S 9 — *St Denys*

Michaelmas Term

S
10

NINETEENTH SUNDAY AFTER TRINITY
Sun rises 7.16, sets 6.16
Oxford Full Term begins

M
11

Tu
12

Michaelmas Term

W 13

Moon's First Quarter, 3.25 a.m.

Th 14

F 15

Dussehra (Hindu)

S 16

Michaelmas Term

S
17

TWENTIETH SUNDAY AFTER TRINITY
St Etheldreda
Sun rises 7.28, sets 6.1

M
18

ST LUKE

Tu
19

Michaelmas Term

W
20

Full Moon, 2.57 p.m.
End of first quarter of Michaelmas Term

Th
21

F
22

S
23

Michaelmas Term

S
24

TWENTY-FIRST SUNDAY AFTER TRINITY
United Nations Day
Sun rises 7.41, sets 5.46

M
25

Tu
26

Michaelmas Term

W
27

VIGIL

Th
28

ST SIMON AND ST JUDE
Moon's Last Quarter, 8.5 p.m.

F
29

S
30

Michaelmas Term

S
31

TWENTY-SECOND SUNDAY AFTER TRINITY
Sun rises 6.53, sets 4.32
Summer Time ends

M
1

ALL SAINTS. Scarlet Day

Tu
2

All Souls

Michaelmas Term

W 3

Th 4
Diwali (Hindu)
New Moon, 9.15 p.m.

F 5
Roll of the Regent House and Lists of Faculties
    promulgated

S 6

Michaelmas Term

S 7

TWENTY-THIRD SUNDAY AFTER TRINITY
Sun rises 7.6, sets 4.20

M 8

Tu 9

Michaelmas Term divides

Michaelmas Term

W
10

Th
11

Moon's First Quarter, 12.46 p.m.

F
12

S
13

Michaelmas Term

S
14

TWENTY-FOURTH SUNDAY AFTER TRINITY
Remembrance Sunday
Prince of Wales born, 1948
Sun rises 7.19, sets 4.9

M
15

Nativity Fast (Orthodox) begins

Tu
16

Michaelmas Term

W 17

Th 18

Guru Nanak Birthday (Sikh)

F 19

Full Moon, 8.57 a.m.

S 20

St Edmund

Michaelmas Term

S
21

SUNDAY NEXT BEFORE ADVENT
Sun rises 7.31, sets 4.0

M
22

St Cecilia

Tu
23

Michaelmas Term

W
24

Th
25

St Catharine of Alexandria

F
26

S
27

Moon's Last Quarter, 12.28 p.m.

Michaelmas Term

S
28

FIRST SUNDAY IN ADVENT
Sun rises 7.42, sets 3.53

M
29

VIGIL
End of third quarter of Michaelmas Term

Tu
30

ST ANDREW

Michaelmas Term

W 1   *St Eligius*

Th 2

F 3   FULL TERM ends

S 4   New Moon, 7.43 a.m.
Oxford Full Term ends

DECEMBER 2021

S
5

SECOND SUNDAY IN ADVENT
Sun rises 7.52, sets 3.48

M
6

St Nicholas

Tu
7

Michaelmas Term

W
8

Th
9

F
10

S
11

Moon's First Quarter, 1.36 a.m.

Michaelmas Term

S
12

THIRD SUNDAY IN ADVENT
Sun rises 8.0, sets 3.47

M
13

Tu
14

Michaelmas Term

W 15

Th 16

O Sapientia

F 17

S 18

Michaelmas Term

S 19

FOURTH SUNDAY IN ADVENT
Full Moon, 4.36 a.m.
Sun rises 8.5, sets 3.48
MICHAELMAS TERM ends

M 20

VIGIL

Tu 21

ST THOMAS

Michaelmas Term

W
22

Th
23

F
24

VIGIL
Library closed

S
25

CHRISTMAS DAY. Scarlet Day
Library closed

Christmas Vacation

DECEMBER 2021

S 26
SUNDAY AFTER CHRISTMAS
ST STEPHEN
Sun rises 8.8, sets 3.52

M 27
ST JOHN THE EVANGELIST
Moon's Last Quarter, 2.24 a.m.
Bank Holiday
Library closed

Tu 28
INNOCENTS' DAY
Bank Holiday
Library closed

W 29
Library closed

Th 30
Library closed

F 31
Library closed

Christmas Vacation

Engagements for JANUARY

MAR.

APR.

Engagements for MAY

MAY

JUNE

JULY

to DECEMBER 2022

2021	S	M	Tu	W	Th	F	S
Oct.	...	...	...	...	...	1	2
	3	4	[5	6	7	8	9
	10	11	12	13	14	15	16
	17	18	19	20	21	22	23
	24	25	26	27	28	29	30
	31						
Nov.	...	1	2	3	4	5	6
	7	8	9	10	11	12	13
	14	15	16	17	18	19	20
	21	22	23	24	25	26	27
	28	29	30				
Dec.	...	...	...	1	2	3]	4
	5	6	7	8	9	10	11
	12	13	14	15	16	17	18
	19	20	21	22	23	24	25
	26	27*	28*	29	30	31	...
2022							
Jan.	...	...	...	...	...	...	1
	2	3	4	5	6	7	8
	9	10	11	12	13	14	15
	16	17	[18	19	20	21	22
	23	24	25	26	27	28	29
	30	30	...	...	...	...	...
Feb.	...	...	1	2	3	4	5
	6	7	8	9	10	11	12
	13	14	15	16	17	18	19
	20	21	22	23	24	25	26
	27	28	...	...	...	...	...
Mar.	...	...	1	2	3	4	5
	6	7	8	9	10	11	12
	13	14	15	16	17	18]	19
	20	21	22	23	24	25	26
	27	28	29	30	31	...	...

Vacations are shown by italic figures.
An asterisk denotes a Bank Holiday.

2022	S	M	Tu	W	Th	F	S
APR.	...	...	...*	...	...	1	2
	3	4	5*	6	7	8	9
	10	11	12	13	14	15	16
	17	**18***	**19**	**20**	**21**	**22**	**23**
	24	**25**	[**26**	**27**	**28**	**29**	**30**
MAY	**1**	**2***	**3**	**4**	**5**	**6**	**7**
	8	**9**	**10**	**11**	**12**	**13**	**14**
	15	**16**	**17**	**18**	**19**	**20**	**21**
	22	**23**	**24**	**25**	**26**	**27**	**28**
	29	**31***	**31**	...	...	...	...
JUNE	...	...	...	**1**	**2**	**3**	**4**
	5	**6**	**7**	**8**	**9**	**10**	**11**
	12	**13**	**14**	**15**	**16**	**17]**	**18**
	19	**20**	**21**	**22**	**23**	**24**	**25**
	26	27	28	29	30	...	..
JULY	...	...	...	...	...	1	2
	3	4	5	6	7	8	9
	10	[11	12	13	14	15	16
	17	18	19	20	21	22	23
	24	25	26	27	28	29	30
	31	...	...	...	...	...	...
AUG.	...	1	2	3	4	5	6
	7	8	9	10	11	12	13]
	14	15	16	17	18	19	20
	21	22*	23	24	25	26	27
	28	29	30	31	...	...	...
SEP	...	...	...	...	1	2	3
	4	5	6	7	8	9	10
	11	12	13	14	15	16	17
	18	19	20	21	22	23	24
	25	26	27	28	29	30	...

First and last days of Full Term and the period for taught courses during the summer are shown by square brackets.

EXAMINATIONS

The Board of Examinations conducts internal Cambridg[e] examinations principally for undergraduates, includ[ing] those for University scholarships, studentships and prizes. Full current information relating, for ex[ample], to guidance to candidates, detailed timetable[s] of examinations (triposes, medical & veterinary, etc.) and of the publication of results, may be found a[t] http://www.admin.cam.ac.uk/students/studentregistry

For information about the admission and examinatio[n] of graduate students studying for the Ph.D., MSc., M.Litt., and other graduate degrees/qualifications se[e] http://www.admin.cam.ac.uk/offices/gradstud/about

UNIVERSITY OFFICERS

Chancellor Lord SAINSBURY.

Vice-Chancellor Prof. S. J. TOOPE.

Pro-Vice-Chancellors Senior Pro-Vice Chancellor Prof[.] G. J. VIRGO (Education), Prof. D. CARDWELL (Strategy &[ ]Planning), Prof. C. ABELL (Research). Prof. A. D. NEEL[Y](Enterprise & Business Relations). Prof. E. V. FERRAN[ ](Institutional & International Relations).

High Steward Lord WATSON.

Deputy High Steward A. M. LONSDALE.

Commissary Rt Hon. Lord JUDGE.

Proctors K. OTTEWELL, A. MONTRESCU-MAYES.

Orator R. J. E. THOMPSON.

Registrary E. M. C. RAMPTON, The Old Schools.

Librarian J. P. GARDNER.

Director of the Fitzwilliam Museum and Marlay Curator L. SYSON.

Executive Director of Development & Alumni Relations A. E. TRAUB.

Esquire Bedells N. HARDY, S. V. SCARLETT.

University Advocate M. H. STEINFELD.

Academic Division The Old Schools. *Academic Secretary*: M. R. W. GLOVER.

Accommodation Syndicate Kellet Lodge, Tennis Court Road. *Secretary*: N. BLANNING.

Careers Service Stuart House, Mill Lane. *Secretary*: J. C. BLAKESLEY.

Institute of Continuing Education Madingley Hall. *Director*: Prof. J. GAZZARD.

Estates Division Greenwich House, Madingley Road. *Interim Director*: G. V. MATTHEWS.

Finance Division The Old Schools. *Director of Finance*: J. D. HUGHES.

Governance and Compliance Division The Old Schools. *Director*: R. B. SACHERS.

Health, Safety and Regulated Facilities Division *Director of Health*: M. VINNELL.

Human Resources Division The Old Schools. *Interim Director*: A. L. E. HUDSON.

Legal Services Division The Old Schools.

Local Examinations Syndicate (Cambridge Assessment) The Triangle Building, Shaftesbury Road. *Group Chief Executive:* S. NASSÉ.

Secretaries of Councils of the Schools Interim appointment of B. A. WARN (*Arts & Humanities*), Interim appointment of M. A. BODFISH (*Biological Sciences*), C. J. EDMONDS (*Clinical Medicine*), J. G. EVANS (*Humanities & Social Sciences*), J. R. BELLINGHAM (*Physical Sciences*), S. T. LAM (*Technology*).

Sports Centre Philippa Fawcett Drive. *Director of Sport:* N. J. BROOKING.

University Press

Chief Executive of the Press and Secretary of the Press Syndicate:
P. A. J. PHILLIPS

Director for People: C. ARMOR; *Chief Financial Officer:* A. P. CHANDLER; *Managing Director, ELT:* P. J. COLBERT; *Managing Director, Academic:* A. M-C. HILL; *Chief Information Officer:* M. C. D. MADDOCKS; *General Counsel:* C. A. SHERET; *Managing Director, Education:* R. H. SMITH; *Director of Syndicate Affairs:* K. J. TAYLOR; *Director of Operations:* M. WHITEHOUSE.

UNIVERSITY LIBRARY

Most University buildings are currently closed in response to the COVID-19 outbreak. Please check online before planning a visit.

For all information about the main University Library see www.lib.cam.ac.uk. For information about affiliated libraries and all other Cambridge libraries, visit the Libraries Gateway at www.lib.cam.ac.uk/camlibraries.

Information about exhibitions at University Library's Milstein Exhibition Centre is available at www.lib.cam.ac.uk/exhibitions.

Information about becoming a Friend of Cambridge University Library is available at www.lib.cam.ac.uk/Friends.

Closure dates (main University Library only)

24 December 2020 – 3 January 2021 inclusive, 2–5 April 2021 inclusive, 30 August 2021, and 24 December 2021 – 2 January 2022 inclusive.

Librarian: J. P. GARDNER.

Cambridge University Library's COVID-19 Collection

The COVID-19 pandemic is unprecedented. As with any historic moment, it is crucial to capture records of the event as it unfolds. Cambridge University Library wants to collect, preserve, and make accessible materials about the effects of the pandemic on the Collegiate University and the city, materials that reflect how people are experiencing this time. How is it affecting daily life, work, social activity, and leisure?

The Library intends collecting materials in physical and digital formats, such as videos, photographs and images (including posters and leaflets), audio recordings, creative projects, as well as journals and diaries. It is also interested in collecting materials published openly online. These websites will be added to the UK Web Archive, which is a collaborative initiative in partnership with the UK's Legal Deposit Libraries.

You can help the Library by sharing your experience of the COVID-19 pandemic.

Contact digitalpreservation@lib.cam.ac.uk to get involved.

MUSEUMS, ETC.

Fitzwilliam Museum

Open to the public Tuesday to Saturday, 10.0–5.0; Sunday and Bank Holidays, 12.0–5.0; closed Mondays, Dec. 24–26, and 31, Jan. 1, and Good Friday.
Reference Library open by appointment.
Telephone 332900; website: www.fitzmuseum.cam.ac.uk
email: reception@fitzmuseum.cam.ac.uk
Director L. SYSON.

Museum of Archaeology and Anthropology

Open Tuesday to Saturday, 10.30–4.30 and Sunday, 12.0 to 4.30. Closed for approximately one week during Christmas/New Year, and on Good Friday and Easter Sunday.
Website: http://maa.cam.ac.uk
email: admin@maa.cam.ac.uk
Curator & Director, Prof. N. J. THOMAS.

Museum of Classical Archaeology

Cast gallery open to the public 10.0–5.0, Tuesday to Friday, Saturday 10.0–1.0. in Term time. (Closed Christmas, New Year, and Easter, and at the discretion of the authorities.)
Telephone, 330402; email, museum@classics.cam.ac.uk

Web: http://www.classics.cam.ac.uk/museum

Director, Y. GALANAKIS to Dec.; Prof. C. VOUT from Jan.

Zoology Museum

Admission is free.

Open Tuesday-Saturday from 10 a.m. to 4.30 p.m. & Sunday from noon to 4.30 p.m. Last admission to the galleries is 4.0 p.m. A café and shop are on site.

The Museum is closed on Mondays, Good Friday and during the Christmas/New Year period.

Telephone: 01223 336650

Email: umzc@zoo.cam.ac.uk

Web: www.museum.zoo.cam.ac.uk

Director, Prof. R. KILNER

The Polar Museum, Scott Polar Research Institute

Open Tuesday to Saturday, Good Friday, and public holiday Mondays, 10.0–4.0. Closed over the Christmas and New Year period. School parties by arrangement. Children must be accompanied by an adult. For further information telephone 336540.

Web: www.spri.cam.ac.uk

Director, Prof. J. A. DOWDESWELL

Sedgwick Museum of Earth Sciences

The Museum is the oldest of the University museums and has a collection of more than two million items. All are welcome and entry is free.

Open Monday to Friday, 10.0–1.0, 2.0–5.0; Saturdays, 10.0–4.0.

Closed Good Friday, Christmas/New Year.

Telephone 333456.

Email: sedgwickmuseum@esc.cam.ac.uk

Web: http://www.sedgwickmuseum.org

Director, E. HIDE.

Whipple Museum of the History of Science

Open Monday to Friday from 12.30 to 4.30. The Museum is closed on public holidays and for a few days at Christmas and Easter. There are also occasional special events on selected evenings and weekends; please consult the website. For further information telephone 330906.

Web: https://whipplemuseum.cam.ac.uk

Curator & Director, Prof. L. TAUB.

Botanic Garden

The Garden now holds more than 8000 plant species. Through the year it hosts events and courses announced on the website.

Admission and Opening Times (entry by Brookside and Station Road Gate).

January, November & December 10.0 a.m.–4.0 p.m.
February, March & October 10.0 a.m.–5.0 p.m.
April to September 10.0 a.m.–6.0 p.m.

An admission charge is made. Please note the Garden is closed from 24 December 2020 to 1 January 2021 inclusive.

Glasshouses and café close half an hour before Garden closing time. Shop closes 15 minutes before Garden closing time. Free admission to undergraduate and post-graduate students of the University upon production of a valid University Card. Last entry is 30 minutes before closing time.

Web: www.botanic.cam.ac.uk

Email: enquiries@botanic.cam.ac.uk

Telephone, 336265

Director, Prof. B. J. GLOVER.

Kettle's Yard, Castle Street

Kettle's Yard House displays modern art and hosts modern and contemporary exhibitions. The new building includes two galleries, a café, shop, welcome area, and a four-floor education wing. Admission is free.

Open Tuesday to Sunday from 11.a.m to 5 p.m.

For forthcoming events and exhibitions see kettlesyard. co.uk

ADC Theatre Park Street

The University playhouse. Two drama productions weekly (evenings) during Term and regular productions at other times.

Web: adctheatre.com; adcticketing.com

The ADC also manages the Corpus Playroom, an 80-seat venue in St Edward's Passage.

Administration, tel. 359547.

Booking, tel. 300085 and online.

Manager, J. RYCROFT.

University Information Services J. J. Thomson Avenue

University Information Services provides IT, research computing and related services including networks, telephones, email, business systems, and a Service Desk for the University and its Colleges. For more information visit https://www.uis.cam.ac.uk/

Opening times for the UIS Reception and the Service Desk can found at

http://www.uis.cam.ac.uk/about-us/service-hours

Enquiries: reception@uis.cam.ac.uk

Director: Prof. I. M. LESLIE.

Telephone: 334600

University Language Centre Downing Place

The Centre promotes and supports language learning for personal, professional, and academic purposes. It offers taught courses for staff and students in a range of languages from absolute beginner to undergraduate level, English for Academic Purposes, support for international students, online and physical resources in over 180 languages, and a personalised advising service to support specific language learning goals. A University Card is required for registration. Non-members of the University may be offered limited access to resources for an annual fee.

The Language Centre is open Mon.–Fri. 9.30–7.30 in Full Term and during CULP teaching weeks, and 9.30–5.30 at other times.

Web: http://www.langcen.cam.ac.uk
Enquiries: enquiries@langcen.cam.ac.uk
Telephone: 335058
Director: J. WYBURD.

(UNIVERSITY OF) CAMBRIDGE STUDENTS' UNION

In a 'Report of the Council on a new students' union' published in the *Cambridge University Reporter, 2019–20* (pp. 370–77), it was proposed to replace the existing Cambridge University Students' Union and Graduate Union with a single body formally to be known as the University of Cambridge Students' Union. The Report was discussed on 17 March and its recommendations were approved by Grace 1 of 27 March 2020.

Cambridge Students' Union, as it is more familiarly known, is the central students' union for all students at all levels of study, at the University of Cambridge. It represents and campaigns on behalf of its members, working hard to improve student experience in all aspects of student life. Led by eight full-time elected officers, Cambridge Students' Union provides a wide range of services and support, which includes printing, binding, and gown sales, as well as supporting clubs and societies. Through the Student Advice Service it is also able to offer confidential, independent advice to any student who needs it.

Telephone: 01223 333 313
Website: www.cambridgesu.co.uk
Facebook: www.facebook.com/yourcambridgesu

NEWCOMERS & VISITING SCHOLARS

The University of Cambridge Newcomers and Visiting Scholars group welcomes newcomers (including post-docs, members of staff, and visiting scholars) and their families, and aims to make their stay in Cambridge enjoyable and successful. It provides a termly programme of events and various interest groups. A welcome morning, usually with a speaker, is held every Tuesday in term time from 10.30 a.m. to 12.0 p.m. at the University Centre.

To register please see: www.nvs.admin.cam.ac.uk or email nvs.enquiries@admin.cam.ac.uk

POSTDOCS OF CAMBRIDGE (PdOC)

Postdocs Of Cambridge is a society which aims to bring together postdoctoral research staff on both a social and an intellectual level and to improve their representation within Colleges and the University. It is open to all postdocs at the University and its Partner Institutions, and includes contract staff who have completed their doctorate but do not have long-term tenure or established positions. The society ensures that information about careers and professional development, college affiliation, and social and welfare provision, is widely disseminated.

Members have regular events, including talks, BBQs, hiking trips, garden and Christmas parties, and meet regularly during the last week of every month at 7 p.m. in a Cambridge pub whose venue is published on the PdOC Society website.

To join the mailing list see www.pdoc.cam.ac.uk
Email: pdoc@admin.cam.ac.uk
Tel: 01223 336741

UNIVERSITY CENTRE

The University Centre is a unique social space for university students, staff, alumni, and their guests. Within the building food can be found in the Main Dining Hall, Grads Cafe, and the Riverside Restaurant (Elior), while award winning wines can be found in the new CUC Wine Bar.

The University Centre, located on Granta Place overlooking the Cam, is more than just a place to eat : there are plenty of areas to relax, catch up on your emails, read the newspapers or study. Facilities at the University Centre include a widescreen TV, Blue Fitness suite, and a number of conference rooms. Lapwing wireless internet is available throughout the building, or members can alternatively obtain a wireless ticket from reception.

The Centre is open from 8a.m. to 11p.m. seven days a week. Further information may be obtained and bookings made as follows:

Main Reception 01223 337766
Conference Services 01223 337796
Email: Conferences@admin.cam.ac.uk
Riverside Restaurant (Elior) 01223 328559
Email: Riverside.Restaurant@elior.co.uk

UNIVERSITY
COMBINATION ROOM

The Combination Room is for the use of current members and retired members of the Roll of the Regent House and their guests. Visiting academics may also be issued with access cards, on nomination by their College or Department.

The Combination Room is open Monday – Friday from 10a.m.to 4p.m.

If you have any queries please email:
ReceptionOldSchools@admin.cam.ac.uk
Old Schools Reception: 01223 332200

DEVELOPMENT AND ALUMNI RELATIONS

The Development and Alumni Relations office is the alumni relations and fundraising arm of the University, responsible for raising major philanthropic gifts and building and sustaining lifelong links between Cambridge and its alumni and supporters across the globe.

Development and Alumni Relations is also responsible for principal alumni engagement programmes including the award-winning alumni magazine *CAM*, digital and e-communications and social media, and the annual Alumni Festival.

Find out about the range of benefits and services available to alumni and former postdocs online at www.alumni.cam.ac.uk and, for those in the USA and Canada, www.cantab.org.

Learn about the fundraising campaign for the University and Colleges at www.philanthropy.cam.ac.uk.

Contact us at:

University of Cambridge Development and Alumni Relations

1 Quayside, Bridge St, Cambridge, CB5 8AB, UK
Telephone, +44 (0)1223 332288
Email: contact@alumni.cam.ac.uk
contact@philanthropy.cam.ac.uk
Website, www.alumni.cam.ac.uk
www.philanthropy.cam.ac.uk

Cambridge in America
1120 Avenue of the Americas 17th Floor, New York, NY 10036, USA

Telephone, +1 212 984 0960
Email: mail@cantab.org
Website, www.cantab.org

COLLEGES, APPROVED FOUNDATIONS, AND APPROVED SOCIETIES

Christ's *Master*: Prof. J. STAPLETON. *Bursar*: D. BALL. *Senior Tutor*: R. HUNT.

Churchill *Master*: Prof. Dame Athene DONALD. *Bursar*: T. JAMES. *Senior Tutor*: R. J. PARTINGTON.

Clare *Master*: LORD GRABINER. *Bursar*: P. C. WARREN. *Senior Tutor*: J. A. TASIOULAS.

Clare Hall *President*: Prof. C. A. SHORT. *Bursar*: I. C. STRACHAN. *Senior Tutor*: I. S. BLACK.

Corpus Christi *Master*: Prof. C. M. KELLY. *Bursar*: to be announced. *Senior Tutor*: M. FRASCA-SPADA.

Darwin *Master*: M. R. W. RANDS. *Bursar*: J. T. DIX. *Dean*: D. J. NEEDHAM.

Downing *Master*: A. P. BOOKBINDER. *Bursar*: G. FLYNN. *Senior Tutor*: G. B. WILLIAMS.

Emmanuel *Master*: Dame Fiona REYNOLDS. *Bursar*: M. J. GROSS. *Senior Tutor*: R. M. HENDERSON.

Fitzwilliam *Master*: Lady MORGAN of HUYTON. *Bursar*: R. G. CANTRILL. *Senior Tutor*: P. A. CHIRICO.

Girton *Mistress*: Prof. S. J. SMITH. *Bursar*: J. S. ANDERSON. *Senior Tutor*: A. M. FULTON.

Gonville and Caius *Master*: P. J. ROGERSON. *Bursar*: R. GARDINER. *Senior Tutor*: A. M. SPENCER.

Homerton *Principal*: G. C. WARD. *Bursar*: D. GRIFFIN. *Senior Tutor*: P. BARTON.

Hughes Hall *President*: A. N. S. FREELING. *Bursar*: V. A. ESPLEY. *Senior Tutor*: P. JOHNSTON.

Jesus *Master*: S. ALLEYNE. *Bursar*: R. F. ANTHONY . *Senior Tutor*: G. T. PARKS.

King's *Provost*: Prof. M. R. E. PROCTOR. *Bursar*: T. K. CARNE. *Senior Tutor*: T. FLACK.

Lucy Cavendish *President*: Prof. Dame Madeleine ATKINS. *Bursar*: L. THOMPSON. *Senior Tutor*: J. GREATOREX.

Magdalene *Master*: Prof. Sir Christopher GREENWOOD. *Bursar*: S. J. MORRIS. *Senior Tutor*: S. MARTIN.

Murray Edwards *President*: Dame Barbara STOCKING. *Bursar*: R. HOPWOOD. *Senior Tutor*: M. GEMELOS.

Newnham *Principal*: A. ROSE. *Bursar*: C. LAWRENCE. *Tutor*: Prof. L. TAUB.

Pembroke *Master*: Lord SMITH OF FINSBURY. *Bursar*: A. T. CATES. *Senior Tutor*: A. W. TUCKER.

Peterhouse *Master*: B. KENDALL. *Bursar*: I. N. M. WRIGHT. *Senior Tutor*: S. W. P. HAMPTON.

Queens' *President*: M. A. EL-ERIAN. *Bursar*: J. SPENCE. *Senior Tutor*: J. W. KELLY.

Robinson *Warden*: A. D. YATES. *Finance Bursar*: F. BROCKBANK. *Senior Tutor*: D. A. WOODMAN.

St Catharine's *Master*: Prof. SIR MARK WELLAND. *Bursar*: N. ROBERT. *Senior Tutor*: H. C. CANUTO.

St Edmund's *Master*: C. E. J. ARNOLD. *Bursar*: E. MURPHY. *Senior Tutor*: J. M. BUNBURY.

St John's *Master*: H. HANCOCK. *Bursar*: C. F. EWBANK. *Senior Tutor*: A. M. TIMPSON.

Selwyn *Master*: R. MOSEY. *Bursar*: M. D. PIERCE. *Senior Tutor*: M. J. SEWELL.

Sidney Sussex *Master*: Prof. R. PENTY. *Bursar*: S. BONNETT. *Senior Tutor*: M. BEBER.

Trinity *Master*: Professor Dame Sally DAVIES. *Bursar*: R. LANDMAN. *Senior Tutor*: Prof. C. S. BARNARD.

Trinity Hall *Master*: J. N. MORRIS. *Bursar*: T. J. HARVEY-SAMUEL. *Senior Tutor*: J. C. JACKSON.

Wolfson *President*: Prof. J. CLARKE. *Bursar*: J. CHEFFINS. *Senior Tutor*: S. LARSEN.

COLLEGE INFORMATION

College websites have a great variety of information that is revised from time to time. Typically they include details of admission, Fellows and staff, alumni, maps, libraries and chapels, current events, historical notes, photographs, societies, and a means of searching the whole archive for specific topics. Colleges also have entries in the online undergraduate and graduate studies prospectuses.

Addresses, all of which follow the standard 'http://www.', and do not admit apostrophes (e.g. Christ's = http://www.christs.cam.ac.uk/) are these:

Christ's	christs.cam.ac.uk
Churchill	chu.cam.ac.uk
Clare	clare.cam.ac.uk
Clare Hall	clarehall.cam.ac.uk
Corpus Christi	corpus.cam.ac.uk
Darwin	dar.cam.ac.uk
Downing	dow.cam.ac.uk
Emmanuel	emma.cam.ac.uk
Fitzwilliam	fitz.cam.ac.uk
Girton	girton.cam.ac.uk
Gonville & Caius	cai.cam.ac.uk
Homerton	homerton.cam.ac.uk
Hughes Hall	hughes.cam.ac.uk
Jesus	jesus.cam.ac.uk
King's	kings.cam.ac.uk
Lucy Cavendish	lucy-cav.cam.ac.uk
Magdalene	magd.cam.ac.uk
Murray Edwards	murrayedwards.cam.ac.uk
Newnham	newn.cam.ac.uk
Pembroke	pem.cam.ac.uk
Peterhouse	pet.cam.ac.uk
Queens'	queens.cam.ac.uk
Robinson	robinson.cam.ac.uk
St Catharine's	caths.cam.ac.uk

St Edmund's	st-edmunds.cam.ac.uk	
St John's	joh.cam.ac.uk	
Selwyn	sel.cam.ac.uk	
Sidney Sussex	sid.cam.ac.uk	
Trinity	trin.cam.ac.uk	
Trinity Hall	trinhall.cam.ac.uk	
Wolfson	wolfson.cam.ac.uk	

MOVABLE FEASTS

	2020–2021	2021–2022
1st Sunday in Advent	Nov. 29	Nov. 28
Ash Wednesday	Feb. 17	Mar. 2
Easter Day	Apr. 4	Apr. 17
Ascension Day	May 13	May 26
Whitsunday	May 23	June 5
Trinity Sunday	May 30	June 12
Corpus Christi	June 3	June 16

A list of movable feasts to the year 2035 may be foun
in *Whitaker's Almanack*, together with full calendars for th
years 1780–2040.

FULL TERMS & GENERAL ADMISSION

2020–2021

Michaelmas: Oct. 6–Dec. 4
Lent: Jan. 19–Mar. 19
Easter: Apr. 27–June 18
　General Admission: 30 June–3 July

2021–2022

Michaelmas: Oct. 5–Dec. 3
Lent: Jan. 18–Mar. 18
Easter: Apr. 26–June 17
　General Admission: 29 June–2 July

2022–2023

Michaelmas: Oct. 4–Dec. 2
Lent: Jan. 17–Mar. 17
Easter: Apr. 25–June 16
　General Admission: 28 June–1 July

2023–2024

Michaelmas: Oct. 3–Dec. 1
Lent: Jan 16.–Mar. 15
Easter: Apr. 23–June 14
　General Admission: 26–29 June

For later dates see the current edition of *Statutes & Ordinances*.

Michaelmas Term begins on Oct. 1 and ends on Dec. 19. Lent Term begins on Jan. 5 and ends on Mar. 25 (or 24 in any leap year, the next being 2024). Easter Term begins on Apr. 10 and ends on June 18, but falls a week *later* whenever Full Easter Term begins on or after Apr. 22, as in the years 2021–2030 inclusive.

THE RIVER

Order of Boats in the Main Divisions, 2020

LENTS

Men's Division 1

1	(2)	LMBC 1	10	(14)	M 1
2	(4)	PEM 1	11	(8)	CTH 1
3	(1)	CAI 1	12	(13)	CL 1
4	(7)	1&3 T 1	13	(9)	CHR 1
5	(3)	DOW 1	14	(11)	PET 1
6	(5)	R 1	15	(16)	Q 1
7	(10)	TH 1	16	(17)	F 1
8	(6)	JE 1	17	(15)	EM 1
9	(12)	K 1			

Women's Division 1

1	(4)	DOW 1	10	(6)	1&3 T 1
2	(2)	JE 1	11	(9)	TH 1
3	(1)	N 1	12	(15)	F 1
4	(3)	EM 1	13	(10)	CHR 1
5	(5)	LMBC 1	14	(17)	Q 1
6	(7)	PEM 1	15	(12)	ME 1
7	(11)	CHU 1	16	(19)	DAR 1
8	(8)	CL 1	17	(16)	CTH 1
9	(13)	CAI 1			

Numbers in brackets show position of boats at start of races.

The MAYS were cancelled for the sake of public health.

INTER-UNIVERSITY CONTESTS, 2019–2020

Many events were cancelled after mid-March for the duration.

Men's Matches

Basketball	Cambridge
Cross Country	Cambridge
Fives (Rugby)	Oxford
Handball	Cambridge
Hockey	Cambridge
Ice Hockey	Cambridge
Judo	Cambridge
Karate	Cambridge
Lacrosse	Oxford
Lightweight Rowing	Oxford
Real Tennis	Oxford
Rugby League	Oxford
Rugby Union	Cambridge
Ski & Snowboard	Cambridge
Squash	Oxford
Table Tennis	Cambridge
Volleyball	Oxford
Water Polo	Oxford

Women's Matches

Basketball	Oxford
Cross Country	Cambridge
Fives (Rugby)	Cambridge
Golf	
Gymnastics	
Handball	Cambridge
Hockey	Cambridge
Ice Hockey	Cambridge
Judo	Oxford
Karate	Cambridge
Lacrosse	Oxford
Netball	Oxford
Real Tennis	Oxford
Rugby Union	Cambridge

Ski & Snowboard	Cambridge
Squash	Oxford
Table Tennis	Cambridge
Volleyball	Cambridge
Water Polo	Oxford

Mixed Teams

Badminton	Oxford
Boxing	Cambridge
Karate	Cambridge
Kendo	Oxford
Korfball	Oxford
Lacrosse	Cambridge
Powerlifting	Cambridge
Swimming	Oxford
Trampoline	Oxford

LONDON TRAINS

At the time of publication it is uncertain what the future pattern of rail services will be. Check before travelling.

The frequency of London trains, and of alterations especially at weekends, make it inadvisable to print the timetables, but space has been left on the following page to enter details.

It is expected that a faster and more frequent service will continue to run to and from King's Cross, with slower trains to and from Liverpool Street. Some trains on the King's Cross route may run across London to Gatwick airport and the south coast, calling at St Pancras International station. The best source of timetable and other information is by accessing the National Rail Enquiries website:

http://www.nationalrail.co.uk, or by telephoning 03457 48 49 50.

Cambridge North station will be convenient for passengers in the north of the city, including the Science Park. There are services to and from King's Cross, Liverpool Street, King's Lynn, and Norwich.

There are also regular train services to Peterborough (for the East Coast main line), Norwich, Ipswich, Stansted Airport, and the Midlands.

It is important to verify train times beforehand; details of forthcoming alterations are available from National Rail Enquiries.

June 2020

LONDON TRAINS

(see note on p. 319)

COACHES

Services were much curtailed from March following government instructions about non-essential travel. Check the websites for developments.

Cambridge to Oxford & to London Airports from Cambridge, Drummer Street/Parkside

For further information please use the following contact numbers and websites, which also give access to other destinations, etc.*

National Express: tel. 08717 818181
Website – www.nationalexpress.com

Oxford

Via St Neots, Bedford, Milton Keynes, Buckingham, and Bicester

Stagecoach Bus: tel. 01234 220030
Website – www.stagecoachx5.com

London Airports

National Express runs coaches from Parkside to Stansted and Luton, and to Heathrow (all terminals) and Gatwick.

National Express also operates an express service to London Victoria Coach Station; it takes about two hours.

* Correct at 9 June

TELEPHONE NUMBERS

The STD code for Cambridge is 01223, prefixed by + 44 from abroad.

University Network

The University Telephone Network is an internal system linking Departments and Colleges. There is a central switchboard (337733) and numbers for most extensions are five digit numbers. Network directories are no longer available, but see

www.cam.ac.uk/email-and-phone-search

Please use the online https://www.lookup.cam.ac.uk

Most extensions are 33xxxx; others are 74xxxx and 76xxxx.

Access codes are still needed for these destinations:

Addenbrooke's Hospital 700
Med. Res. Council (LMB) 145

University Departments, etc.

332200	Academic Division
338099	Accommodation Service
334396	African Studies Centre
356942	Air Squadron
217889	Anaesthesia, Division of
335079	Anglo-Saxon, Norse, & Celtic, Dept. of
765000	Applied Mathematics and Theoretical Physics, Dept. of
765040	Applied Research in Educational Technologies, Centre for (CARET)
333538	Archaeology, Dept. of
333516	Arch. and Anth., Museum of
332950	Architecture, Dept. of
333147 333148 }	Archives
766222	Arts & Humanities, School of
766886	Arts, Social Sciences & Humanities, Research Centre for

Colleges
With postcodes

334900	Christ's CB2 3BU
336000	Churchill CB3 0DS
333200	Clare CB2 1TL
332360	Clare Hall CB3 9AL
338000	Corpus Christi CB2 1RH
335660	Darwin CB3 9EU
334800	Downing CB2 1DQ
334200	Emmanuel CB2 3AP
332000	Fitzwilliam CB3 0DG
338999	Girton CB3 0JG
332400	Gonville and Caius CB2 1TA
747111	Homerton CB2 8PH
334898	Hughes Hall CB1 2EW
339339	Jesus CB5 8BL
331100	King's CB2 1ST
332190	Lucy Cavendish CB3 0BU
332100	Magdalene CB3 0AG
762100	Murray Edwards CB3 0DF
335700	Newnham CB3 9DF
338100	Pembroke CB2 1RF
338200	Peterhouse CB2 1RD
335511	Queens' CB3 9ET
339100	Robinson CB3 9AN
338300	St Catharine's CB2 1RL
336250	St Edmund's CB3 0BN
338600	St John's CB2 1TP
335846	Selwyn CB3 9DQ
338800	Sidney Sussex CB2 3HU
338400	Trinity CB2 1TQ
332500	Trinity Hall CB2 1TJ
335900	Wolfson CB3 9BB

Miscellaneous

359547	ADC Theatre
245151	Addenbrooke's Hospital, General Enquiries
217118	Accident & Emergency
01245 493131	Anglia Ruskin University
496000	Babraham Institute
741251	Blackfriars
221400	British Antarctic Survey
457000	Cambridge City Council
101	Cambridge City Police
767787	Cambridge Theological Federation
01223 706050	Cambridge Water Company (day and night)
768740	Conference Cambridge
311545	East Asian History of Science Library (Needham Research Institute)
742192	Fisher House
315084	Joint Colleges Nursery Linkline
267000	Molecular Biology (M.R.C. Laboratory)
233258	Nat. Inst. of Agric. Botany (NIAB)
744444	Nightline
303336	Nuffield Hospital
0300 303 5303	Open University
0845 7484950	Railway Inquiries
245888	Rape Crisis Centre, Cambridge
746580	Ridley Hall
364455	Samaritans, Cambridge
350365	Student Community Action
337575	Varsity Newspaper
741033	Wesley House
741000	Westcott House
330633	Westminster College

Websites

For Colleges see pp. 313–14.

The URL of the University Web server is http://www.ca̶
.ac.uk/. This has links to Departmental, College, and ot̶
specialised servers. Some useful links are:

University web search: http://search.cam.ac.uk
Email & phone search (including University-only search)
    http://www.cam.ac.uk/email-and-phone-search
University Map:
    http://www.cam.ac.uk/map
University Telecoms Office:
    http://www.phone.cam.ac.uk
University Reporter:
    http://www.admin.cam.ac.uk/reporter
Statutes & Ordinances:
    http://www.admin.cam.ac.uk/univ/so
University Library: http://www.lib.cam.ac.uk
University Offices: http://www.admin.cam.ac.uk
University Information Services: http://www.uis.cam.ac.uk̶
Other servers in the University:
    http://www.cam.ac.uk/university-a-z